Report Form Roundup

Written by Linda Milliken
Typography and Design by Lorraine Ste[g]
Edited by Kathy Rogers
Cover Design by Wendy Loreen
Cover Art by Patty McCloskey

D0129066

Reproducible for classroom use on[ly].
Not for use by an entire school or school system.

Contents

Report From Roundup • ©1998 Edupress • PO Box 883 • Dana Point, CA 92629
ISBN 1-56472-068-3
Printed in USA

Teaching Information

Report Form Roundup presents reports on three different levels so that students can improve writing and fact-collecting skills.

The three levels (A, B, and C) are described below. The contents page indicates the level of each report form.

LEVEL A:
Reports are based on personal experiences or use simple resource materials such as newspapers. Writing skills: listing of facts, simple sentence building.

LEVEL B:
Reports include an assignment checklist and report worksheet. Resource materials include the encyclopedia and various media. Writing skills: listing of facts, building sentences and short paragraphs. Includes topic suggestions and one additional report requirement.

LEVEL C:
Reports include an assignment checklist, fact-gathering worksheet and one-page written report form. Students will gather facts, then incorporate those facts into a more complete written project. Includes topic suggestions and additional report requirements.

Autobiography

This is the story of your life!

Full Name _____

Date of birth _____ City of birth _____

Birth weight _____ Birth length _____

Age today _____ Grade _____

I have attended these schools _____

_____

The school I attend now is _____

Current address _____

_____

My first memory _____

_____

Two other memories

1. _____

_____

2. _____

_____

Vacations I have taken _____

_____

My biggest accomplishment _____

_____

My favorite stuffed animal (name and description) _____

_____

My hobbies _____

_____

3

My Family

Meet my family. These people are important in my life.

My name is _____

List names of everyone living in your household including parents, brothers, sisters, other relatives and extended family. Write their relationship to you after each name.

_____

_____

_____

List *four other* relatives not named above. Write their relationship to you after their name.

1. _____

2. _____

3. _____

4. _____

Some relatives live in cities other than your own. List as many of those cities as you can.

_____

_____

List *three* important family dates and the reason for their celebration. These could be birthdays, anniversaries, or traditional events.

Date	Event
_____	_____
_____	_____
_____	_____

Our favorite family holiday is _____

The thing we like best to do together is _____

Family Photo Album

Glue a photo in each box. If you don't have photos, draw pictures.
If you have an especially large family, add more paper.

This is me.
My name is _____.

Meet my relatives.

The relative I especially enjoy is

The relative I think you would like is

Report Form Roundup © *Edupress*

My School

Name of school _____

Address *(street)* _____

     (city, state) _____

Date built _____

What is the meaning behind the school name? Why was it chosen?

_____

Name of principal _____

Name of vice-principal _____

Name of secretary _____

Number of teachers _____ Number of students _____

Number of classrooms _____ Grades taught _____

List the buildings, rooms and areas on the school grounds other than classrooms.

For example: office, auditorium, computer lab, playground

_____

_____

Write *two* sentences describing different areas of your school.

1. _____

2. _____

In the space below, draw a map of your school. Label all buildings and areas. Color your classroom red.

My Classroom

School _____

Teacher _____ Room number _____

Count the number of each below and write the total next to the item.

windows _____   doors _____   desks _____

chairs _____   bulletin boards _____   closets _____

chalkboards _____   centers _____   sinks _____

flags _____   books _____   calendars _____

Describe one bulletin board _____

_____

Describe one center _____

_____

List *six* words that describe your classroom (hints—*colorful, cozy, bright, noisy, quiet, etc.*).

_____

_____

In the space below, draw a diagram of the inside of your classroom. Be sure to
include and label everything.

Color the desk you sit at red.

Report Form Roundup © *Edupress*

Hobby Report Checklist

A hobby is something you enjoy doing over and over again in your spare time. It might be collecting things or it might be an activity. Maybe you will find your hobby (or one you would like to start) in the lists below.

Collection

dolls   stamps
miniature cars   rocks
stickers   model airplane
posters   baseball cards
shells
stuffed animals
marbles

Activity

dancing   gymnastics
puppet shows   arts and crafts
birdwatching   reading
fishing   photography
writing pen pals
training pets
learning about cars

Check the box when you complete each task.

☐ Choose the hobby for your report. If you have a hobby report on that one. If you don't have a hobby find someone who does and report on that.

☐ Complete the Hobby Report form.
- If you are reporting on a **collection** answer questions marked **A**.
- If you are reporting on an **activity** answer questions marked **B**.
- Answer all questions in complete sentences.

☐ Project: Choose one from the list below (or do more for extra credit).
- Bring a sample of your collection to share and describe to your classmates.
- Draw a picture of you doing your free time activity.
- Demonstrate your activity to the class.
- Bring a sample of something you made in your free time.

Hobby Report

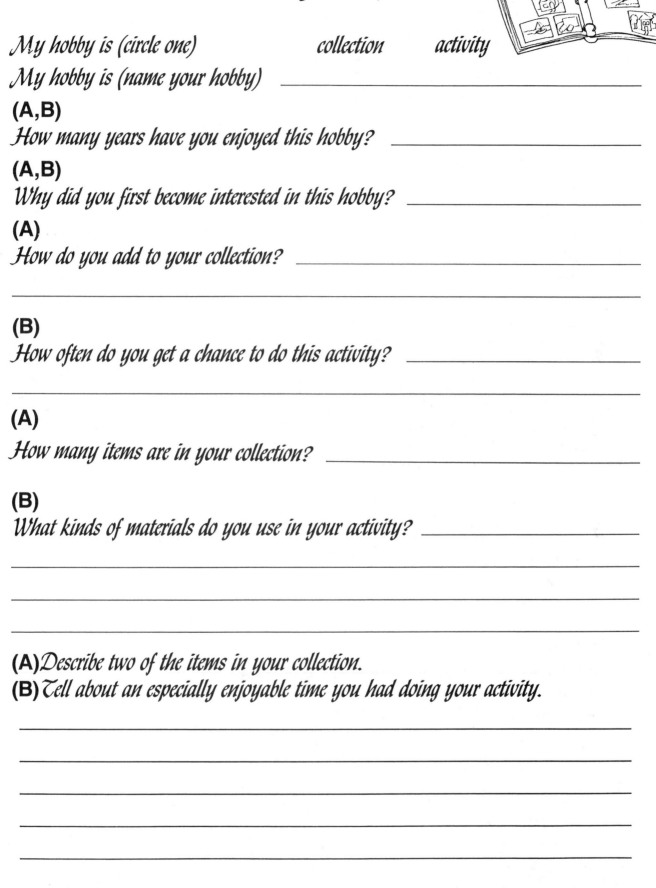

My hobby is (circle one)   collection   activity

My hobby is (name your hobby) _____

(A,B)

How many years have you enjoyed this hobby? _____

(A,B)

Why did you first become interested in this hobby? _____

(A)

How do you add to your collection? _____

_____

(B)

How often do you get a chance to do this activity? _____

_____

(A)

How many items are in your collection? _____

(B)

What kinds of materials do you use in your activity? _____

_____

_____

(A) Describe two of the items in your collection.

(B) Tell about an especially enjoyable time you had doing your activity.

_____

_____

_____

_____

_____

Report Form Roundup © Edupress

My Favorite Holiday

Name of holiday _____

Date celebrated _____

Reason for celebration _____

_____

Is this an official state or national holiday (or both)? _____

On what date was this offically made a holiday? _____

How is this holiday celebrated (traditions, events, activities)? List one for each category.

• National _____

• State _____

• Local _____

• Personal _____

What colors are associated with this holiday? _____

_____

List any songs associated with this holiday. _____

_____

_____

List any symbols associated with this holiday. (Look at the border on the page for help.)

_____

_____

_____

Local Current Event

Most communities have a newspaper that reports on events and people in that town or city. Your report should be based on a story from one of these local newspapers.

Newspaper _____

Date of Publication _____

Communities covered by reports _____

_____

How often is this newspaper published?(Circle the correct choice)

daily   weekly   bi-weekly   monthly

Other _____

Story headline _____

Reporter's name _____

Circle the word or words that best describe the content of the report.

political   business   human interest   criminal   sports

Other _____

Who is the report about? _____

When did the news event take place? _____

Where did the news event take place? _____

What happened? Write three sentences that summarize what you read in the news report.

1. _____

_____

2. _____

_____

3. _____

Why do you think this was a newsworthy story? _____

Cut out the current event and clip it to this report.

Front Page News

The front page of a newspaper has local, national and international news articles. Select a *major* newspaper (not a local one). Read the headlines. Choose an article for your report. Cut out the article and any pictures that go with it. Staple them to your report.

Name of newspaper _____

Date _____ **Edition** _____

Write the headline in **BIG, BOLD** letters.

Reporter's name _____

A front page story usually begins with the location of the news event. In what city, state and/or country did the event take place?
_____

List three people mentioned in the article. Write their job or position after their name.

1. _____

2. _____

3. _____

The article will probably be continued on another page. Be sure to read and cut out *all* of it. Write a summary of the information in the news article.

_____

_____

_____

_____

_____

_____

Current Event Report — Sports

By _____

Name of Newspaper _____

Date (Day, Month, Year) _____

Section and Page of Article _____

Headline _____

Reporter's Name (if given) _____

Where did the event take place?

What sport was involved?

When did the event take place?

What teams (if any) were taking part in this event?

If the article is about a certain athlete, what is his or her name?
If the article is about teams, list several players mentioned.

_____

Write a few sentences summarizing the event.

_____

_____

What do you think was the most important thing that happened during the game or event?
(This could be the turning point that led to victory or defeat.)

_____

_____

Cut out the article and any picture that was with it and staple it to this report.

Report Form Roundup © *Edupress*

WEATHER REPORT

These weather words should help:

clear, cloudy, overcast, foggy, stormy, windy, hazy, breezy, bright, sunny, warm, cold, chilly, freezing, blizzard, rain, hail, sleet, hot, calm, dry

Describe the weather conditions throughout the day.

Morning (before noon):

sky _____ sun _____ wind _____

temperature _____ changes _____

Put that information into a sentence or two to describe the weather conditions during the morning hours.

_____

_____

Afternoon (noon until 5:00 p.m.)

sky _____ sun _____ wind _____

temperature _____ changes _____

Put that information into a sentence or two to describe the weather conditions during the afternoon hours.

_____

_____

Evening (5:00 p.m. until morning):

sky _____ sun _____ wind _____

temperature _____ changes _____

Put that information into a sentence or two to describe the weather conditions during the evening hours.

_____

_____

Check the newspaper or listen to television or radio newscasts to gather information about temperatures and forecasts for the coming days.

Tomorrow's forecast _____

_____

National Weather Report

Look in the newspaper weather
section for this information.

Newspaper _____

Date of weather report _____

Report

The highest temperature was _____ in the city of _____.

The lowest temperature was _____ in the city of _____.

List *four* cities where the **highest** temperature was *over* 70^0.

_____

_____

List *four* cities where the **lowest** temperature was *under* 60^0.

_____

_____

List two cities that had the weather conditions listed below.

• **rain** _____

• **snow** _____

• **thunderstorms** _____

Forecast

What words would describe the forecast (expected weather in different parts of the country)?

• **east** _____

• **west** _____

• **central** _____

Report Form Roundup © *Edupress*

Movie Review

Look in the entertainment section of a newspaper for some of this information.

Name of movie

Producer

Director

Starring _____

_____

Co-starring _____

_____

Circle as many of the words below that describe the movie.

adventure   *mystery*   *romance*   *comedy*

drama   *cartoon*   *thriller*   *tear-jerker*

Do you think the title is a good one? Tell why or why not.

_____

_____

Did you like the main character in the movie? Tell why or why not.

_____

_____

Would you want to see the movie again? Tell why or why not.

_____

_____

Has this movie been nominated for any awards?

_____

_____

On a scale of 1 to 10, how would you rate this movie? _____

Television Show Review

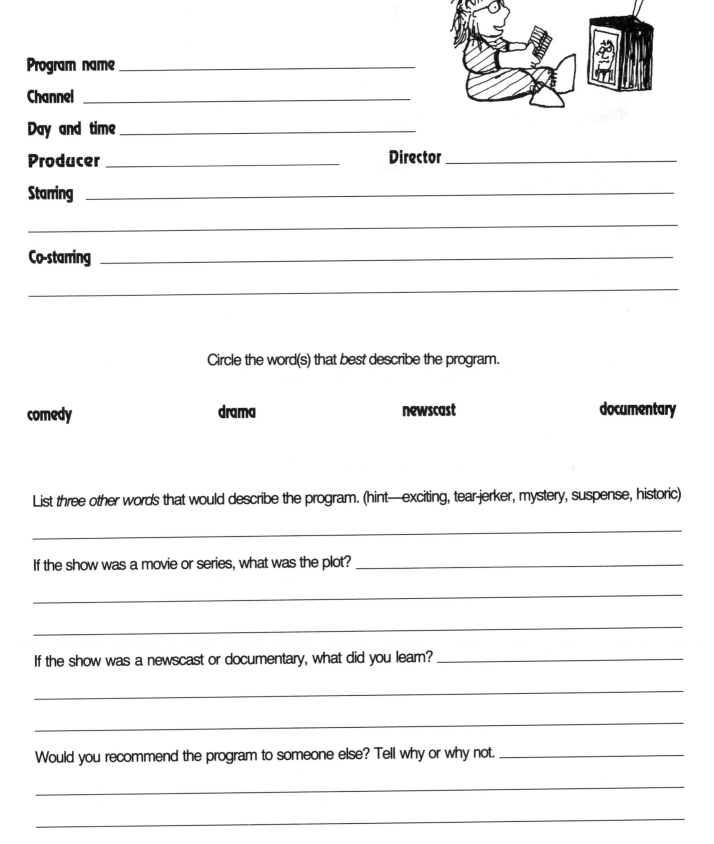

Program name _____

Channel _____

Day and time _____

Producer _____ Director _____

Starring _____

_____

Co-starring _____

_____

Circle the word(s) that *best* describe the program.

comedy   **drama**   **newscast**   **documentary**

List *three other words* that would describe the program. (hint—exciting, tear-jerker, mystery, suspense, historic)

_____

If the show was a movie or series, what was the plot? _____

_____

_____

If the show was a newscast or documentary, what did you learn? _____

_____

_____

Would you recommend the program to someone else? Tell why or why not. _____

_____

_____

Report Form Roundup © *Edupress*

Restaurant Review

By _____

The name of the restaurant I am reviewing is _____.

This restaurant serves: (circle the choices)

Breakfast   Lunch   Dinner

The restaurant hours are:

OPEN AT _____

CLOSED AT _____

The menu offers: (list at least five items)

Does the restaurant have food "to go"?
YES   NO

If you eat here I recommend you try:

The last time I ate there I had:

Describe the inside of the restaurant.

Would you recommend this restaurant to a friend? Why? Why not?

Some restaurants have sample menus for their customers to take home. I was able to get one and it is attached to this report.   ☐

I was not able to get one. ☐

Visit My Community

If you came to visit my community
I would want you to see a special place.

Place _____

Location _____

Circle the word or words that best describe this place.

amusement park   recreation area   restaurant
viewpoint   local landmark   historical landmark

Other _____

Cost of admission _____

Hours open _____

Two things we could do there

1. _____

_____

2. _____

_____

Two things we would see there

1. _____

_____

2. _____

_____

One interesting fact about this place _____

_____

Clothes to wear _____

One souvenir you should get is _____

_____

Report Form Roundup © Edupress

Community Newsletter

A newsletter is a short form for a newspaper. It reports information about a subject like a business or a hobby.

You are going to write a newsletter about your community. Just use the newsletter worksheet and be sure to check the box when you finish each step.

☐ **Name Your Newsletter**
There is room at the top to print the name you have chosen for your newsletter. Here are some suggestions. (Pretend the name of the community is Great Place.)

News from Great Place   *Great Place Hotline*
What's Happening?   *Tidbits from Great Place*

☐ **News Sections**
There are three sections for reporting news—People, Sports and Exciting News. Be sure to write in complete sentences and include names, places, scores and any other important information you have gathered.

You can write about personal news or check the local newspaper for information.

☐ **Around Town**
You need to choose three people and ask them a question. Be sure to have note paper ready when you ask so you can copy their answer. Then write the newsletter information from your notes. Be sure to include the name of the person you interviewed. For example: "I like living in Great Place because it has nice stores." (Joan Little)

☐ **What's at the Movies?**
You will need to check the listings in your local newspaper. List the name of the movie, the name of the theater and the time the movie can be seen on the correct lines.

☐ **You Must See This!**
Think of the most interesting, special or amazing things in your community. If a visitor came, you would want to show him this. What is the place and where is it located?

A newsletter report about my community.

By _____

The name of my community is _____.

People News

Sports News

Around Town

I asked three people this question: "What do you like best about living here?"
This is what they said:

1. _____

2. _____

3. _____

Exciting News

You Must See This!

Places to Eat

1. _____

2. _____

3. _____

What's at the Movies?

Name of movie: _____

Where playing: _____

Times shown: _____

Report Form Roundup © *Edupress*

Interview Checklist

An interview is very simple. You select a person and ask questions! You should always be prepared. Have your questions ready before you begin an interview.

Follow the steps below to gather your information and write the interview report. Check the box when you finish each step.

☐ **Pick a Person to Interview**
The answers may surprise you even if you decide to interview someone you know well.

☐ **The Interview**
Find a comfortable spot to have your interview. Be sure to have a copy of the Interview Notes (the questions are prepared for you) and a sharpened pencil ready.

Write the answers next to the questions. When you take notes you do not write complete sentences. You write "key" words that will help you remember what the person said.

☐ **Write the Interview Report**
Fill in the person's name at the top. Check to make sure you have spelled the *first and last* names correctly. Use your notes to help you complete the report.

● Fill in each blank line with the correct pronoun or information necessary. You do not need to use the person's first *and* last name each time they are mentioned in the interview.

● The report is divided into paragraphs. Each will have the information from a question you asked. Read the topic sentence, then use your notes to write sentences to complete the paragraph.

If possible, attach a picture of the person interviewed to the report.

Interview Notes

When you interview someone ask the questions slowly and clearly.
You do not need to write the answers in complete sentences.
You will do that when you write the interview report.

QUESTIONS:

1. Please spell your first and last name.

   _____

2. What is your best quality? _____

   _____

   Why do you think this is your best quality? _____

   _____

3. Tell me about something you especially enjoy doing. _____

   _____

   _____

4. What is your favorite book? _____

   What is your favorite song? _____

   What is your favorite movie? _____

   What is your favorite color? _____

5. Tell me about your most special memory.

   _____

   _____

   _____

An Interview With _____

While interviewing _____ I learned some interesting things I would like to
first and last name

share on this report. _____ thinks _____ best quality is
name   his/her

_____.

_____ feels this is _____ best quality because _____
He/She   his/her

_____.

_____ especially enjoys _____
name

When asked to name _____ favorite things _____ thought for a
his/her   name

moment and then answered:

_____

_____

Although _____ has many wonderful memories _____ most
name   his/her
special is:

_____

_____

Fiction Book Report

Title _____

Author _____

Publisher _____

List *three* words that would describe the book. (Hint: *scary, funny, exciting, romantic, sad, silly, adventure*)

_____

_____

List at least two characters in the book. _____

_____

Describe one of these characters. _____

_____

_____

Which character would you want to be? Why? _____

_____

_____

Write *three* sentences, each describing a different event in the book.

1. _____

_____

2. _____

_____

3. _____

_____

If you could *rename* the book what title would you choose? _____

Report Form Roundup © *Edupress*

Non-Fiction Book Report

Title _____

Author _____

Publisher _____

What was the subject of the book? _____

Circle the words that best describe the information in the book.

plant   animal   land   water   outerspace

Other _____

What is the most *unusual* fact you learned about the subject? _____
_____

List *four* other facts you learned about the subject.

1. _____

2. _____

3. _____

4. _____

Write *four* new words you learned relating to the subject. Write the meaning of each.

1. _____

2. _____

3. _____

4. _____

Mystery Book Report

Title _____

Author _____

Publisher _____

What was the mystery that needed to be solved?

_____

_____

Which character (or characters) solved the mystery?

_____

What were two clues that helped solve the mystery?

1. _____

2. _____

What recognition or reward was given for solving the mystery?

_____

_____

Tell about one exciting adventure that took place.

_____

_____

_____

Were you surprised at the solution to the mystery? Tell why or why not.

_____

_____

Report Form Roundup © *Edupress*

Fairy Tale Report Checklist

A fairy tale is a story of fantasy and make-believe. It often tells of fairies, elves, pixies and imaginary beings with magical powers. It can also tell a tale that teaches a lesson.

Check the box as you finish each task.

☐ *Choose a fairy tale for your report.*

Aladdin and the Wonderful Lamp
The Seven Voyages of Sinbad
The Ugly Duckling
Sleeping Beauty
The Shoemaker and the Elves
Little Red Riding Hood
Rumpelstiltskin

Rapunzel
Snow White
Jack and the Beanstalk
Tom Thumb
Puss-in-Boots
Cinderella
Hansel and Gretel

☐ *Complete the Fairy Tale Report.*

- **Country of origin**—where was this story written?
- **Author**—if there is no author write "adapted."
- **Characters**—tell whether the magical powers were good or evil and what these powers were. If there were no characters with magical powers pick an unusual character to describe.
- **Lesson**—was there a "moral" to the story or a lesson to be learned?
    For example—*"Never trust a stranger in the woods!"*

☐ *Project:* Choose one of the following.

- Make a puppet based on a character in the tale.
- Make a poster that advertises the fairy tale.
- Bring a copy of the tale to class and read it aloud to your classmates.

Fairy Tale Report

Name of fairy tale _____

Country of origin _____

Author _____

Characters.

List the main characters. _____

_____

- Describe the powers of a magical character OR describe an unusual character.

_____

_____

Choose a feeling listed below and tell about the part of the story that made you feel that way.

scared   excited   surprised   happy   unhappy   worried   nervous

_____

_____

_____

Tell about the most *imaginary* part of the story.

_____

_____

_____

_____

Did anyone live "happily ever after?" Who? Why did they live "happily ever after?"

_____

_____

What lesson did the fairy tale teach? _____

_____

_____

Report Form Roundup © *Edupress*

Legend Report Checklist

A legend is a popular folk tale that is passed on through books, stories and literature. Most legends tell about people, places and events. Some are based on real persons but many are imaginary characters. Complete your legend report by following the assignment checklist below.

☐ Choose a name from the list of legendary people for your report.

American Legends
Paul Bunyan
Pecos Bill
Casey Jones
Daniel Boone
Davy Crockett
Mike Fink
Buffalo Bill
John Henry
Johnny Appleseed
Pocahontas
Annie Oakley

British Legends
Sir Galahad
Davy Jones
Beowulf
Sir Lancelot
Peter Pan
Robin Hood
Dick Wittington
King Arthur

You will need to use the encyclopedia and books about the legendary person or folk tales to help you write your report.

☐ Complete the report form.

Background
Write a few sentences telling about where this character was born and raised, what he or she liked to do and what jobs he or she had.

Qualities
Heroes of legends have unusual or admirable qualities. After you have learned about the subject of your report, what qualities did you most admire?

Daring feat
Heroes of legends have done some remarkable things. Their accomplishments are admired and remembered by many. Tell about something accomplished by the hero in your report.

☐ Attach a picture of the legendary character to your report. You can draw it yourself or trace it from a book.

An Interesting Legend

By _____

Name of legendary character

Country of origin

Is this character real or imaginary? _____

What is the background of the real-life character?

_____

_____

_____

If the character is imaginary, how did the legend get started?

_____

_____

What unusual or admirable qualities did this legendary person have?

_____

_____

Describe a daring feat or heroic act this person performed.

_____

_____

_____

_____

Athlete Report Checklist

Sports fans all over the world enjoy watching and cheering on their favorite athletes. Find out more about these athletes who have provided so much excitement through the years.

Check the box as each task is completed.

❏ Choose an athlete for your report.

You may select a name from the list below or research an athlete, either past or present, of your own choosing.

Ben Hogan	*Bobby Jones*	*Jack Nicklaus*	*Sam Sneed*
Arnold Palmer	*Leo Durocher*	*Dizzy Dean*	*Lou Gehrig*
Cy Young	*Henry Aaron*	*Casey Stengel*	*Ty Cobb*
Jim Thorpe	*Jesse Owens*	*Wilma Rudolph*	*Babe Didrikson*
Jackie Robinson	*Connie Hawkins*	*Mickey Mantle*	*Satchel Paige*
Connie Mack	*Wilt Chamberlain*	*Oscar Robinson*	*Fran Tarkenton*
Bill Russel	*Vince Lombardi*	*Muhammad Ali*	*Joe Namath*
Knute Rockne	*John Unitas*	*Sonny Liston*	*Rocky Marciano*
Helen Wills	*Rod Laver*	*Richard Petty*	*Louis Chevrolet*

❏ Complete the Athlete Report form.

Biographical facts—List two personal facts (childhood, parents, educations, etc.).

Chronological events—Write a short paragraph of three sentences that list, in the order that they happened, different events in this athlete's career.

Highlights and accomplishments—List two outstanding achievements. These could be "best season" statistics, specific tournament or game highlights.

Records—All sports keep records and statistics of players' accomplishments. List any record that the athlete held or holds.

Current or retirement information—What is the player doing now? What did the player do after retiring?

❏ Project

Choose **one** of the following (or do both for extra credit).

• Make a "Table of Important Career Dates." On notebook paper write these headings:

Date	Event	Importance

List information in chronological order under each column heading.

• If you are reporting on an athlete currently in the news, clip out articles and paste them in a scrapbook to share with your classmates.

Athlete Report

Name of Athlete _____

Personal Information

Date born _____

Place of birth _____

Present age OR age at death _____

Two biographical facts

1. _____

_____

2. _____

_____

Career information

Sport played _____

Three chronological events

1. _____

2. _____

3. _____

Career highlights and accomplishments

1. _____

_____

2. _____

_____

Records _____

_____

Championships and awards won _____

_____

Present activities or activities after retirement _____

_____

World Leader Report Checklist

Every country in the world has leaders. These people have a great deal of power and influence. Some are leaders of state while others head the government. Many of them have fascinating stories to tell of their years in power.

Check the box as you complete each task.

☐ **Choose a world leader for your report.**

This person can be someone presently in power or you can dig into history and find someone from the past for your report.

The titles below are some of the positions of leadership held throughout history. In order to find a person for your report, pick a country, find the article in the encyclopedia and read the section on history. You will find many names from which to choose. You will probably need to get more information from library books.

Chancellor
Czar
Emperor
Empress
Kaiser
King
Queen
Prince
Pharoah
Premier
President
Prime Minister
Sultan
Rajah

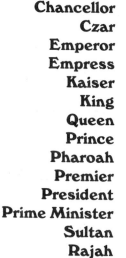

☐ Complete the World Leader Report Form

General Information—title means president, chancellor etc.—list the dates and number of years in office or power. You will find the length of time in power will be quite different for each leader.

Personal Information—list birth and death dates plus three other facts about this leader's life other than those years he or she was in power.

Career Information—Circle the word that best tells how this person gained his or her power. If the correct word is not listed fill in the line below.

Events during leadership—describe three changes or world events during this person's time in power. What is this leader most famous for—this could be a personal or career fact not already listed.

Leadership Qualities—Write two words that would describe this person's qualities or characteristics as a leader. Words to help you—fair, tough, respected, shrewd, incompetent, competent. You will find other "word-hints" in your research reading.

☐ Project

Pretend you are the leader of a country. Make a **word-collage** showing the qualities and characteristics **you** would have as a leader.

Cut letters from magazines. Paste them together to make these words. Cover a piece of 11x17-inch construction paper.

World Leader Report

Name _____

Title _____

Leadership   Country governed or ruled _____

Number of years _____ Dates _____

Personal Information

Date of birth _____ death _____

Other interesting facts

1. _____

_____

2. _____

_____

3. _____

_____

Career Information   Circle the word that tells how this leader came into power:

elected   **inherited**   **military coup**

Other _____

Events during years in power

1. _____

_____

2. _____

_____

3. _____

_____

Most famous for _____

_____

Leadership qualities and characteristics _____

_____

Report Form Roundup © *Edupress*

BIOGRAPHY REPORT CHECKLIST

A BIOGRAPHY IS THE STORY OF A PERSON'S LIFE WRITTEN BY SOMEONE ELSE. YOU ARE GOING TO BE THAT "SOMEONE ELSE." YOU WILL DISCOVER INTERESTING INFORMATION ABOUT A PERSON'S LIFE, PERSONALITY AND INFLUENCE ON OTHERS.

CHECK THE BOX AS YOU COMPLETE EACH TASK.

☐ CHOOSE A PERSON FROM THE LIST BELOW FOR YOUR REPORT.

LEONARDO DA VINCI	JOAN OF ARC	GALILEO	CHARLES DICKENS
LOUIS PASTEUR	SOCRATES	JULIUS CAESAR	MARIE CURIE
THOR HYERDAHL	PAUL GAUGUIN	JOHANN STRAUSS	FLORENCE NIGHTINGALE
THOMAS EDISON	PETER PAUL RUBENS	BENJAMIN FRANKLIN	JACQUES-YVES COSTEAU
EL GRECO	SIR ISAAC NEWTON	MICHELANGELO	LUDWIG VON BEETHOVEN
CONFUCIUS	CAPTAIN JAMES COOK	HENRI MATISSE	JOHANNES GUTENBERG
FERDINAND MAGELLAN	MARCO POLO	NAPOLEON	ROBERT EDWIN PEARY
NOSTRADAMUS	ARISTOTLE	MARK TWAIN	ALEXANDER THE GREAT
JOHANN BACH	ERNEST HEMINGWAY	COLUMBUS	WILLIAM SHAKESPEARE

☐ COMPLETE THE BIOGRAPHY FACT SHEET.

The fact sheet information is the guide to your report. Each fact requested should be easy to understand. Be sure to include dates, ages and important events that helped shape this person's life and goals.

☐ COMPLETE THE BIOGRAPHY REPORT.

- Write information from box **A** on the fact sheet into sentences to complete paragraph **A** on the report form.

- Do the same for boxes **B**, **C**, and **D**.

- Paragraph topic sentences are written for you.

☐ PROJECT

Make a **Time Line** showing the important events in the person's life.

You will need a long strip of butcher paper (about 12 inches wide by 4 feet long). Begin on the left with the person's birthdate. Every 6 inches add a new event continuing until death (or the present if person is not deceased). You may illustrate the events if you want. The sample below will help.

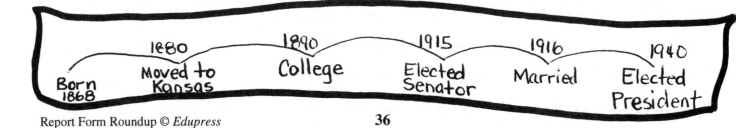

BIOGRAPHY FACT SHEET

A — GENERAL INFORMATION

PERSON _____

DATE OF BIRTH _____

PLACE OF BIRTH _____

CIRCLE THE WORD OR WORDS THAT BEST DESCRIBE THIS PERSON

inventor	explorer	scientist	author	artist	composer
philosopher	adventurer	politician	statesman	military leader	religious leader

Other _____

B — EARLY LIFE

- INTERESTS _____

_____

- EDUCATION, SKILLS, TRAINING _____

_____

_____

- TWO OTHER EARLY LIFE FACTS

1. _____

_____

2. _____

_____

C — ACCOMPLISHMENTS

- BEST KNOWN FOR _____

_____

- OTHER ACCOMPLISHMENTS _____

_____

_____

D — LATER YEARS (INCLUDE DATE OF DEATH IF DECEASED.) _____

_____

BIOGRAPHY REPORT

A — I WOULD LIKE TO INTRODUCE YOU TO _____ .

name

_____

_____

_____

_____

B — IN THE EARLY YEARS _____ WAS INTERESTED IN _____

name

_____ .

SKILLS AND EDUCATION INCLUDED: _____

_____

_____

THERE WERE OTHER IMPORTANT EVENTS. _____

_____

_____

_____

_____

C — _____ WAS A PERSON WHO ACCOMPLISHED MANY THINGS. _____

name

_____

_____

_____

_____

D — DURING THE LATER YEARS OF _____ LIFE _____

name   he/she

_____

_____

_____

_____

State or Province Report Checklist

A state or province is a political and geographic division within a country. Each has its own government and boundaries. But more than that, each state and province has symbols, climate, landmarks and history that are uniquely its own.

Check the box as you finish each task.

☐ **Choose a state or province for your report.**

There are 10 provinces in Canada and 50 states in the United States. Choose one of these for your report. You will find complete listings in the encyclopedia under each country.

☐ **Complete the State or Province Fact Sheet.**

General information—These should be clear as to what information is requested. The origin of the name is usually from another language or culture. Be sure to list this plus the meaning of the name.

Identifying symbols—Each state has its own state or provincial symbols. You will find this information uder "state facts" in the encyclopedia. List *three* products or industries.

Historical facts—List and describe *two* historical events that occurred either before or after statehood or entering the dominion. Include dates.

Places to visit—Where could we go…what could we see if we were to visit? You can list historical landmarks, museums, important buildings or interesting places to see. Tell why we would want to go there.

Features—List names of at least *three* physical features (names of rivers, mountains, types of land, elevations, etc.). Describe the climate year-round (high and low temperatures, types of weather).

☐ **Complete the State or Province Report.**

Paragraph headings match headings on the fact sheet. Rewrite your research information into paragraphs under each heading. Be sure each begins with a topic sentence.

For example, the Places to Visit paragraph might begin—
"California has many interesting places to visit."

☐ **Project**

Make a state or province notebook. It must include the following pages:
- report fact sheet
- drawing of flower or emblem
- report form
- any pictures or articles you can find
- drawing of flag
- drawing of state seal or provincial coat of arms with a paragraph describing it

Report Form Roundup © *Edupress*

State or Province Facts

General Information   Circle one: State   province

Name of state or province _____

Country (United States or Canada) _____

Meaning and origin of name _____

Date granted statehood or entered dominion _____

Population (include date of last census) _____

Size in relation to other states or dominions _____

Identifying symbols

Flower or emblem _____

Motto _____   Song _____

Chief products _____

Historical Facts

1. _____

_____

2. _____

_____

Places to visit

1. _____

_____

2. _____

_____

3. _____

_____

Features

Physical _____

_____

Climate _____

_____

State or Province Report

General Information

_____

_____

_____

_____

_____

Identifying Symbols

_____

_____

_____

_____

Historical Facts

_____

_____

_____

_____

Places to Visit

_____

_____

_____

_____

Features

_____

_____

_____

_____

Report Form Roundup © _Edupress_

Country Report Checklist

The term "country" means a nation with its own name and geographical boundaries. There are about 170 independent countries in the world. Each has its own traditions, history and interesting facts.

Check the box as you complete each task.

☐ **Choose a country for your report.**

Look under the continent headings for lists of country names.
The continents are: Europe, Asia, Africa, North America, South America, Antarctica, and Australia (which is a country in itself).

☐ **Complete the Country Report Fact Sheet.**

General information (Box A)—country name and name of continent on which it is found, list bordering countries, size in square miles or kilometers, population and date of last census, elevation, languages spoken and form of government.

Geographical features (Box B)—include names of rivers, mountain ranges, deserts, climate, plant life.

History (Box C)—list two historical facts.

People and culture (Box D)—include facts about traditions, lifestyle, background.

Products and Resources (Box E)—list the natural resources and tell how the people use them.

☐ **Complete the Country Report form.**
Rewrite the information from each box on the fact sheet after the corresponding letter on the report form. The topic sentence is written for you. Make sure your sentences are complete and make sense.

☐ **Project:** Complete one of the following (or do both for extra credit).

• Be a tour guide. Make a scrapbook listing interesting places a customer might visit. Include pictures cut from magazines or travel brochures.

• On large poster board sketch and paint or color the map of the country.

Country Report Fact Sheet

A — General Information

Country _____   Continent _____

Size _____   Elevation _____

Population _____   Language _____

Government _____

Bordering countries _____

B — Geographical Features

_____

_____

_____

_____

C — History

1. _____

_____

2. _____

_____

D — People and culture

1. _____

_____

2. _____

_____

E — Products and resources

_____

_____

_____

_____

Report Form Roundup © *Edupress*

Country Report

A — _____ is a country located on the continent of

_____

_____

_____

_____

B — Mother Nature has created many geographical features in this country.

_____

_____

_____

C — Learning about its history helps you to understand more about the country of

_____

_____

_____

D — The people and cultural traditions are interesting. _____

_____

_____

_____

E — Chief products and natural resources include _____

_____

_____

_____

Desert Report Checklist

Deserts cover about one-seventh of the earth's land area. Most are in warm climates. They have a wide variety of land formations, plants and animals.

Check the box as you complete each task.

☐ **Choose a desert for your report.**

Arabian
Australian
Colorado
Death Valley
Gobi
Great Basin
Great Salt Lake
Great Victoria
Kalahari

Kara Kum
Kyzyl Kum
Libyan
Mojave
Negev
Painted
Sahara
Syrian
Thar

☐ **Complete the Desert Fact Sheet.**

Location—List the countries, states or provinces the desert covers. List any oceans or landmarks the desert borders.

Size—List area (square miles or kilometers and distance covered north to south, east to west). List one interesting fact about the size.

Land description—List and describe *three* physical features (dunes, oases, plateaus, rocks, etc.).

Climate—List the words that generally describe the desert climate (hot, dry, dusty, windy, etc.) List the average rainfall and the temperature range in degrees.

People—Write two factual sentences about any people who live in or visit this desert.

Animal life—List at least *three* animals that can be found in this desert.

Plant life—List at least *three* interesting facts about the plant life (what kind, how do they grow, etc.).

☐ **Complete the Desert Report.**

Look for key words from your fact sheet in each paragraph instruction. Use the facts to write complete sentences.

☐ **Project**
Draw a map showing the area covered by the desert. Staple the map to your report.

Report Form Roundup © *Edupress*

Desert Fact Sheet

Name of desert _____

Location _____

_____

Size _____

_____

Land description

1. _____

_____

2. _____

_____

3. _____

_____

Climate   descriptive words _____

average rainfall _____   temperature range _____

People   1. _____

_____

2. _____

_____

Animal life   _____

_____

Plant life   1. _____

_____

2. _____

_____

3. _____

_____

Desert Report

Introduction

Include name, location and size information in this paragraph.

_____

_____

_____

_____

Landscape and Climate

Include land description and climate information in this paragraph.

_____

_____

_____

_____

Desert Dwellers

Include information about the people who live in the desert.

_____

_____

_____

_____

Animals of the Desert

Include information about animal life in this paragraph.

_____

_____

_____

_____

Plant Life

This paragraph should include information about plant life.

_____

_____

_____

Report Form Roundup © *Edupress*

Continent Report Checklist

A continent is a part of the earth's surface that forms a great land mass. It usually has plains, plateaus and mountains. A continent is completely or nearly surrounded by water. But that's just the beginning. You will learn much, much more from your research on the seven continents of the world.

Check the box as you complete each task.

☐ **Choose a continent for your report.**

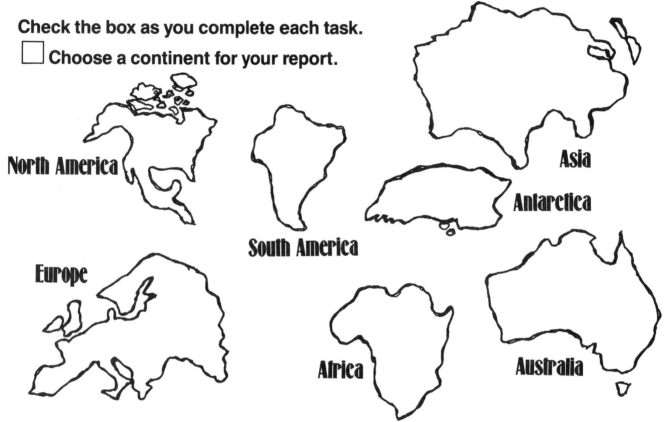

North America

South America

Europe

Africa

Asia

Antarctica

Australia

☐ **Complete the Continent Report form.**

• **General information**—list area, population, density in square miles or kilometers. List elevation in feet or meters.

• **Physical features**—Choose three from the list. Write the name of one found on the continent. For example: river—Nile, Niger.

• **People**—You will find many facts about the people. Decide on two for your report. This could include information about religion, work and lifestyle.

• **Language**—Several languages may be spoken on the continent. List as many as you can.

• **Historical facts**—Choose two interesting historical facts and write them in complete sentences.

☐ **Project**

Choose **one** from the list below. (Or do more for extra credit.)

• On poster board, draw a map of the continent. Label countries and surrounding oceans and seas. Draw and label major rivers, lakes and mountain ranges.

• Make a collage of animal life found on the continent. Draw or cut out magazine pictures and paste them to poster board. Label the animals.

• Others in your class will be researching the same continent. Choose a partner and compare your information. Make an oral presentation to the class.

Continent Report

Continent _____ **Area** _____

Size in relation to other continents _____

Elevation   highest _____   lowest _____

How many independent countries are on this continent? _____

List at least three of them. _____

_____

Name the bodies of water that border this continent:

_____

_____

Physical features

mountain   river   lake   desert   glacier   ice shelf   jungle   forest

1. _____

2. _____

3. _____

List two facts about the people living on this continent.

1. _____

_____

2. _____

_____

List three kinds of animal life found on this continent. _____

_____

Write two historical facts about this continent.

1. _____

_____

2. _____

_____

   Report Form Roundup © *Edupress*

Mountain Report Checklist

Mountains cover about one-fifth of the land surface of the world. Some lie below the seas and others rise thousands of feet or meters above sea level. Learn more about these majestic and fascinating creations of nature.

Check the box as you complete each task.

☐ Choose a mountain from the list for your report.

Mount Whitney
Mount Logan
Mount Hood
Mount Fuji
Mount Rainier
Mount Makalu
MountAssiniboine
Mount Kilimanjaro
Krakatoa
Vesuvius
Cotopaxi

Mount Etna
Mount Everest
Mount McKinley
Mount Shasta
Mount Cook
Matterhorn
Mont Blanc
Mauna Loa
Mauna Kea
Annapurna

☐ Complete the Mountain Report form.

- **General information**—name of mountain and range of which it is a part, height in feet and meters, geographic location (where is it?), type (folded, faultblock, dome or volcanic).

- **Nickname**—have the local people or mountain climbers given the mountain any other name? If yes, what is it and why did they choose that nickname?

- **Features**—list the land formations found on the mountain—canyons, valleys, ice cliffs, glaciers, etc. Describe the plant life and climate.

- **Facts**—write two more interesting facts about the mountain in complete sentences. These facts could include information on scientific experiments, unusual features, size in relation to other mountains in the world and history.

- **Use**—tell how people use the mountain—farming, mining, climbing, scientific research, etc.

- **Choice**—choose one of the suggestions and write a *paragraph*.

☐ Project

Choose a method and make a replica of the mountain. You may:
- draw on poster board

- make a clay, plaster or salt/flour model

Mountain Report

Name _____

Range _____ Type _____

Location _____

Was the mountain named for someone? If yes, who and why? _____

_____

Nicknames _____

_____

Features

• Land _____

_____

• Plant life _____

_____

• Climate _____

_____

Other interesting facts

1. _____

_____

2. _____

_____

How do people use the mountain? _____

_____

Choice: Write a paragraph that describes one of the features or events on the mountain.

mountain climbing expedition   volcanic eruption   animal life

_____

_____

_____

Natural Wonders

The world we live in provides us with countless spectacular sights. From the highest waterfall to the deepest crater... from the densest jungle to the most barren ice shelf... you will be amazed at what you learn about Mother Nature's handiwork!

❑ **Check the box as you complete each task.**

Choose a natural wonder for your report. Each place is listed under the name of the continent on which it is found.

North America
Bay of Fundy
Columbia Icefields
Grand Canyon
Carlsbad Caverns
Everglades
Bryce Canyon
Yellowstone Falls
Old Faithful
Death Valley
Mammoth Cave
Arches National Park
Rainbow Natural Bridge
Giant Sequioa Trees

Africa
Victoria Falls
Nile River
Ngorongo Crater
Dead Sea
Great Rift Valley

Australia
Great Barrier Reef
Coral Reef
Ayers Rock

Antarctica
Ross Ice Shelf
Liv Glacier

South America
Rio Negro
Amazon Jungle
Amazon River
Angel Falls
Iguazu Falls
Cotopaxi
Andes

Asia
Himalayas
Vale of Kashmir
Lake Baykul
Yangtze River
Ganges River

Europe
Alps
Vatnajokoll
Geiranger Fjord
Eisriesenwelt
Mount Erebus
Kverkjokull

❑ **Complete the Natural Wonders Report form**

Location—On which of the seven continents will we find this natural wonder? In which country? If your report is on a river, you may need to list several countries, provinces, or states.

Description—Describe type (waterfall, river, volcano, lake, etc.), list length, width, depth, height, and any other description of size that applies.

History—Write two sentences that tell about the history of this natural wonder. For instance, how or when was it formed, when was it discovered, when or how was it explored? What historic events took place on, or were caused by, this work of nature?

Features and facts—List a feature or fact about this natural wonder that best fits the descriptive word.

Visiting—How could we visit the location of this natural wonder? Would we need to fly, backpack, go on a boat, etc.? Write a short paragraph.

❑ **Project:**

Draw a map of the continent on which this natural wonder is found. Show its location on the continent. Rewrite the feature and fact information in complete sentences on the map.

Natural Wonder Report

Name of natural wonder _____

Location
Continent _____

Country or countries _____

_____

States/provinces/regions _____

_____

Description
Type_____

Size _____

_____

History
1. _____

_____

2. _____

_____

Plant and animal life _____

_____

Features and facts
amazing_____

_____

interesting_____

_____

unusual _____

_____

impressive_____

_____

Visiting this natural wonder

_____

_____

CAPITAL CITY CHECKLIST

Every country in the world has a capital city. Here you will find the government that runs the country and many things of cultural and historical interest.

Check the box as each task is completed. ★★★★★★★★★★★★★

☐ **Choose a city for your report. You may choose from the list below or find one on your own.**

Manila	Jerusalem	Paris	Dublin
Baghdad	San Juan	Jakarta	Washington DC
Lisbon	New Delhi	Warsaw	Copenhagen
Lima	Athens	Edinburgh	London
Bonn	Santiago	Vienna	Budapest
Canberra	Rome	Buenos Aires	San Salvador
Cairo	Kabul	Ottawa	Brussels

☐ **Complete The Capital City Fact Sheet.**

General Information

• **Nickname**—some cities have been given another name. For example, Paris is also called the "city of lights." Explain why a city has earned that nickname.

• **Historical facts**—list two events that have taken place since the founding of the city.

• **Landmarks**—these could be historical sites, buildings, monuments, museums, etc.

• **Places to visit**—other than the landmarks listed, where else of interest would someone go? What would they see?

☐ **Complete the Capital City Report.**

Match the fact boxes (each has been given a letter A, B, C, D or E) to the corresponding paragraphs on the report form. Topic sentences have been written for you. Be sure to rewrite the factual information in complete sentences when writing the paragraphs on the report.

☐ **Project:**

Make a capital city scrapbook about five pages in length. Include pictures, a map of the city and any other articles, information or pictures you can find.

CAPITAL CITY FACTS

A. – GENERAL INFORMATION :

City _____ Country _____

Nickname and reason for nickname _____

_____

Population _____

Area covered _____ Altitude _____

B – TWO HISTORICAL FACTS:

1. _____

_____

2. _____

_____

C – LANDMARKS:

1. _____

_____

2. _____

_____

3. _____

_____

D – PLACES TO VISIT:

1. _____

_____

2. _____

_____

E – WOULD YOU LIKE TO VISIT THIS CITY? WHY OR WHY NOT?

_____

_____

_____

   Report Form Roundup © *Edupress*

CAPITAL CITY REPORT

A ➥ Welcome to _____ in the country of

city

_____

country

_____

_____

_____

B ➥ _____ has an interesting history. _____

city

_____

_____

_____

C ➥ When you visit _____ you will see many land-

city

marks. _____

_____

_____

_____

D ➥ _____ also has many other wonderful sights and

city

places to visit. _____

_____

_____

_____

E ➥ As your travel guide I recommend that you _____

_____

_____

Musical Instrument Report

For a list of musical instruments look under music in the encyclopedia. Select one instrument for your report.

Name of instrument _____

Family   (Circle the correct family.)

brass   wood wind   keyboard

string   percussion   other

History

Write three sentences that tell the history of this instrument.

1. _____

2. _____

3. _____

Description

• shape, materials, size _____

_____

• parts _____

Features

List *two* features similar to other instruments in the same family.

1. _____

2. _____

List *two* features that make it different from other instruments in the same family.

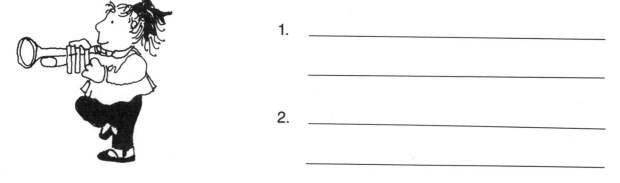

1. _____

_____

2. _____

_____

Sport Report Checklist

People enjoy playing and watching sports. Your research will teach you more about a sport you may already enjoy or one you're not familiar with.

Check the box as you finish each task.

☐ **Choose a sport from the list for your report.**

jai alai	squash	scuba diving	croquet
baseball	basketball	bowling	football
golf	tennis	soccer	rugby
racquetball	polo	volleyball	skiing
waterpolo	boxing	fencing	surfing
weightlifting	skydiving	horseshoes	canoeing
waterskiing	wrestling	fishing	ice skating
table tennis	swimming	mountain climbing	badminton

☐ **Complete the Sport Report form.**

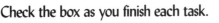

- Historical facts—Include facts about how the game and equipment have changed, associations that have formed, etc.
- Equipment—List the necessary equipment for both playing and safety.
- Terms—There are many words associated with a sport. Pick two to list and define. For example: *flutter kick—swimming kick that alternates legs up and down.*
- Goal—What do the athletes have to do to win?
- Scoring—How does a player or team score? (This includes point scoring and timed results.)
- Officials—How many and what are their titles?
- Championships or awards—List any major championships in which the teams or athletes compete.
- Abilities—In *your* opinion, what skills or talents does an athlete need to do well in this sport?
- Some helpful words—*strength, speed, balance, concentration, flexibility, weight, muscles*

☐ **Project:** Choose *one* from the list below.

- Draw a large diagram of the playing field, course or court. Label the parts and show the dimensions.
- Demonstrate the sport to your classmates. For example, bring a golf club and balls and show how to hit the ball. Compare the different clubs.

Sport Report

Name of sport _____

Team or individual sport _____

History

Where did the sport begin? _____

_____

When did the sport begin? _____

_____

Two other historical facts

1. _____

_____

2. _____

_____

Equipment

Playing _____

_____

Uniform _____

_____

Circle the words that best tell where the game is played:

indoor   outdoor   land   air   water   court   course   field

Other _____

Terms: List and define two associated with this sport.

1. _____

2. _____

Goal _____

Scoring _____

Officials _____

Championships _____

Abilities needed _____

Report Form Roundup © *Edupress*

Bird Report Checklist

Did you know . . . no other animal can travel faster than a bird . . . all birds have wings but not all can fly? Learn these and other interesting facts in your bird report research!

Check the box as you complete each task.

☐ **Choose a bird for your report.**
There are over 8500 kinds of birds so you may choose from the list below or check "Bird" in the encyclopedia for more names.

Blue jay	Wren	Sandpiper	Bluebird
Oriole	Heron	Cardinal	Meadowlark
Mockingbird	Owl	Falcon	Hummingbird
Woodpecker	Flamingo	Parrot	Albatross
Roadrunner	Pelican	Eagle	Sparrow
Canary	Cockatoo	Macaw	Bobolink

☐ **Complete the Bird Report Form.**

- Family—Name the scientific classification.

- Length—List in inches or centimeters.

- Coloring—Describe the coloring for each category.

- Bird call—Describe the sound the bird makes when it sings.

- Names—List any other names or nicknames.

- Eating habits—What does the bird eat? What unusual habits does the bird have getting or eating its food?

- Nest—List the materials used in building the nest. Where are the nests built?

- Eggs—How many does the female lay? Describe coloring and size.

- Location, migration—Geographic area where bird can be found. Tell where it travels during the year.

- Facts—List three facts about the bird that aren't in the information already reported.

☐ **Project:**

Make a bird display. Include the following:

- Magazine picture or drawing of the bird.

- Nest sample—build one yourself! Try to gather the same materials the bird uses.

- Egg sample—draw a picture or paint a hardboiled egg.

Be prepared to tell others about the items in your display.

Bird Report

Bird _____

Family _____

Coloring:

• Young _____

• Adult male _____

• Adult female _____

Song or bird call: _____

Names:

• Nicknames or other names _____

• Reason for nickname or other name _____

Nest:

• Materials _____

• Location _____

Eating habits: _____

_____

Eggs:

• How many _____

• Description _____

Location, migration: _____

_____

Three interesting facts:

1. _____

_____

2. _____

_____

3. _____

_____

Insect Report Checklist

Insects form the largest group of animals on earth. These small, six-legged creatures are among the most successful of the world's organisms at adapting, changing, and surviving in almost every possible climate.

Check the box as you complete each task.

☐ **Complete the Insect Report form.**

General information—name of insect, scientific family, approximate size in inches or millimeters, expected lifespan, habitat (where would we find this insect?), names of other types of this same insect.

Benefits—tell why the insect is either harmful or a benefit to man.

Description—list four *physical* features that describe this insect.

Survival—describe how the body structure, breathing, sense of touch, hearing, etc., help the insect survive.

Living habits— write a short paragraph that gives information about how this insect lives (eating, sleeping, biting etc.)

Other facts—list any unusual facts about the insect other than the ones already reported.

☐ **Project**

Build a model **or** draw a diagram of the insect in your report.

Insect Report

name _____

family _____

approximate size _____

natural habitat _____

lifespan _____

Other types _____

Benefits _____

_____

description _____

_____

_____

Survival capabilities _____

_____

_____

living habits _____

_____

_____

_____

_____

three other facts

1. _____

_____

2. _____

_____

3. _____

_____

Flower Report Checklist

Scientists estimate there are about 250,000 kinds of flowers and flowering plants throughout the world. Your research will teach you more about nature's colorful gift to the world!

Check the box as each task is completed.

☐ **Choose a flower for your report.** You may select from the list or check the encyclopedia under "Flower" for more choices.

sweet pea	morning glory	carnation
forget-me-not	foxglove	four-o'clock
black-eyed Susan	bluebonnet	bluebell
acacia	gardenia	poinsettia
thistle	venus' flytrap	ragweed
Indian pipe	snapdragon	tiger lily
pansy	petunia	tulip

☐ **Complete the Flower Fact Sheet.**
- Family—this is a scientific classification.
- Origin—look up information on the history of the flower.
- Facts—find facts not already included in the rest of the report.

☐ **Write the Flower Report.**

The fact sheet has a symbol at the beginning of each fact. Match the fact symbols with the paragraph symbols on the report form. Use the information on the fact sheets to write the paragraphs. The topic sentence is already written for each paragraph.

☐ **Project:**

Make a flower chart. Glue the items listed below onto a large poster board.
- a hand-drawn color picture of the flower
- seed samples, if available
- magazine pictures of the flower
- any other pictures, articles or information you can gather

EXTRA CREDIT—Try to find seeds for the flower and grow a sample.

Flower Fact Sheet

- **Name of flower** _____
- **Family** _____
- **History** _____

_____

Where was this flower originally grown? _____

Where is it grown now? _____

How did the flower get its name? _____

_____

★ Description

stem _____

height _____

shape _____

colors _____

❀ List three other facts about the flower.

1. _____

_____

2. _____

_____

3. _____

_____

Report Form Roundup © *Edupress*

Flower Report

● There are over 250,000 flowering plants and flowers. This report is about the

_____

_____

_____

_____

_____

_____

★ Try to picture this flower in your mind as I describe it in words. _____

_____

_____

_____

_____

_____

_____

❀ There are several other interesting facts about this flower. _____

_____

_____

_____

_____

_____

_____

Animal Report Checklist

Scientists have classified one million kinds of animals. Many new varieties are discovered annually. They range in size from microscopic protozoans to the enormous blue whale. No matter which animal you research, you will learn some amazing things.

Check the box as you complete each task.

☐ **Choose an animal for your report from one of the groups.**

Animals of the . . .	Animals of the . . .
deserts	oceans
mountains	grasslands
temperate forests	tropical forests
polar regions	

Check the encyclopedia under "Animal" for complete listings.

☐ **Complete the Animal Fact Sheet.**

- **General information**—include animal name, type (wild or domestic), physical features.

- **Living Habits**—how does the animal survive on a daily basis?

- **Environment**—research the animal and its environment . . . how has it changed, how does the animal adapt, etc.

  List ways the animal defends itself—camouflage, armor, hiding, playing dead, burrowing, poison, etc.

- **Other facts**—list other interesting features or facts about the animal not already reported.

☐ **Complete the Animal Report.**

Match the information headings on the fact sheet to the information headings on the report form. Rewrite the facts in complete sentences to make a paragraph under each heading. Remember to start with a topic sentence. For example, The lion has learned to adapt to its environment.

☐ **Project:**

Choose one of the following (or do both for extra credit).

- Make a picture collage of the animal in your report. Hunt through magazines and old picture books. Then paste the pictures to posterboard.

- If the animal in your report is a domestic pet keep a chart on the care and feeding of the animal. Record your observations in a notebook.

Report Form Roundup © *Edupress*

Animal Fact Sheet

General Information

Name _____

Type _____ Expected lifespan _____

Natural Habitat _____

Height _____ Weight _____

Physical features _____

_____

Living habits

Types of food eaten _____

Obtains food by _____

_____

Type of home and how it is built _____

_____

Care of its young _____

_____

Environment

How has the animal adapted to its environment? _____

_____

Means of defense _____

_____

Other interesting facts

1. _____

_____

2. _____

_____

3. _____

_____

Animal Report

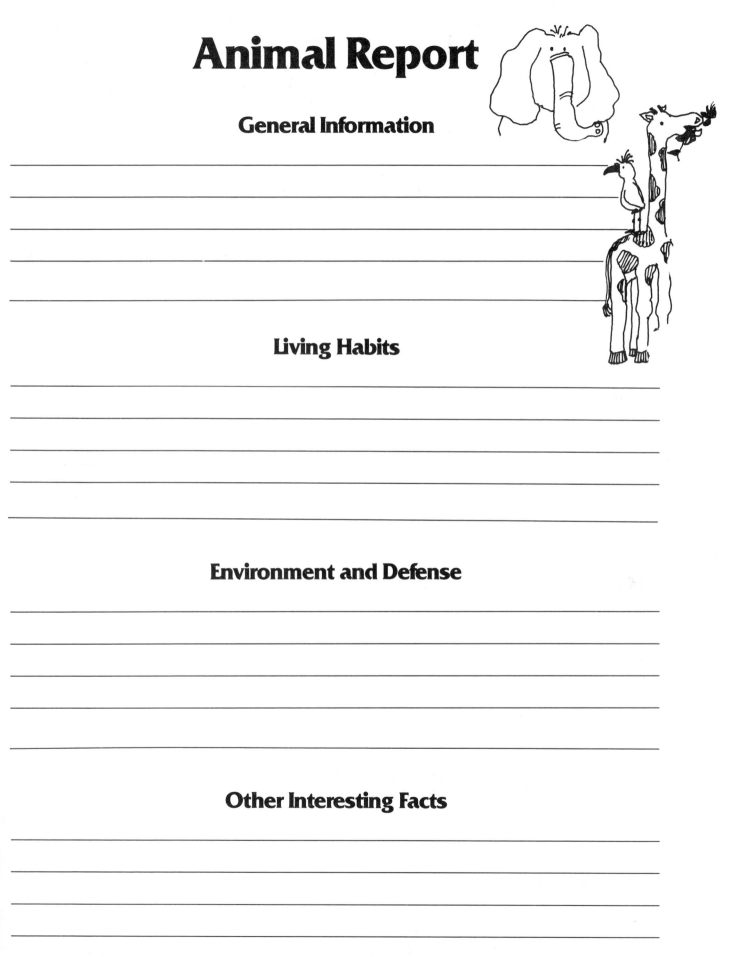

General Information

_____

_____

_____

_____

_____

Living Habits

_____

_____

_____

_____

_____

Environment and Defense

_____

_____

_____

_____

_____

Other Interesting Facts

_____

_____

_____

_____

Report Form Roundup © _Edupress_

𝓟𝓛𝓐𝓝𝓔𝓣 *Report Checklist*

☐ There are eight other planets besides Earth in the solar system. Choose one from the list below for your report.

Pluto	Neptune	Uranus	Saturn
Venus	Mars	Mercury	Jupiter

☐ **Fill in the Planet Report Form.**

● **Planet Facts**—This information can be found in the World Book Encyclopedia.

● **More Information**—The encyclopedia will also give you this information. You can also check books about the solar system or the planet you have chosen. Write your answers in the form of a list.

● **Planet Life, Planet Surface**—This information can also be found in the encyclopedia or library books. This information should be written in complete sentences.

● **Opinion**—This should be based on the facts you have gathered. Be sure to write a complete sentence.

☐ **Report Additions**

If you found a picture of the planet of your choice in a book or encyclopedia, sketch, color or paint the planet and attach the artwork to your report.

THE PLANET _____

PLANET FACTS

By _____

Diameter _____

Number of satellites _____

Average temperature _____

Discovered by _____

Distance from sun _____

Closest distance from Earth _____

Position to sun in solar system _____

MORE INFORMATION

List other things scientists know about this planet.

1. _____

2. _____

3. _____

4. _____

PLANET LIFE

Is there any life form on this planet? _____

If "yes," what kind? _____

_____

PLANET SURFACE

Describe the surface of the planet.

OPINION

What do you think is the most unusual thing about this planet?

THE FUTURE

Tell about any past or planned space programs involving this planet.

Report Form Roundup © *Edupress*

Invention Report Checklist

Choose an invention to be the topic of your report. Because there have been thousands of inventions throughout history, you will find lists below from which to choose. Read the sections, then pick one that sounds interesting to you.

Medical

Stethoscope
Thermometer
X-Ray Machine
Hypodermic Syringe

Transportation

Locomotive
Bicycle
Steamboat
Automobile
Airplane
Helicoper

Science

Magnetic Compass
Microscope
Telescope
Transistor
Laser
Radar

Communication

Radio
Telephone
Telegraph
Television
Typewriter
Satellite
Motion Picture

Home & Family

Food Canning
Sewing Machine
Vacuum Cleaner
Electric Light
Photography
Phonograph

Everyday

Paper
Zipper
Cellophane
Wheel
Glass
Rubber
Aluminum

Completing the Invention Report Form

Now you are ready to fill in the information on the report form. The report is divided into five sections. Some require listing information; others ask you to write short paragraphs.

The report also asks you to gather some samples and draw some pictures. Attach these to your Invention Report Form to make your job complete!

Getting the Information

You will need to use some resources to fill in your report form. The encyclopedia is always a good place to start. You can also go to the library for books on inventions and on the topic that you have chosen.

Report Additions

Make a 4-page scrapbook about this invention. Here are some things you can include:

A sample of the invention
Pictures of the invention, catalogs, samples of the invention in use
Newspaper or magazine clippings either telling about the invention or showing the invention being used

Invention Report

Name of Invention _____ By _____

History

Date first invented _____ Date Patented _____

Name of inventor (if known) _____

Country where invented _____

Changes

All inventions change through the years as improvements are made. Write three sentences describing the changes in this invention.

_____

_____

_____

_____

_____

Uses

List as many ways as you can that this invention can be used.

_____

_____

_____

_____

_____

Importance

Do you think this is an important invention? Tell why or why not.

_____

_____

_____

Report Form Roundup © *Edupress*

Oral Report

How-to demonstration

When you give an oral presentation you need to be very organized. You also need to practice!

☐ Choose a topic for your demonstration

Look at the list below for ideas. You may choose a demonstration from the list or think of your own.

Make a peanut butter and jelly sandwich
Draw a picture
Make soapsuds and blow bubbles
Weave a placemat
Plant a seed
Pitch a pup tent
Wrap a present

Beat an egg white
Make a paper airplane
Make paper flowers
Build a model
Do a leaf rubbing
Tie different knots
Serve a tennis ball

☐ Complete the Oral Report Organizer

As you work be sure you are doing the "how-to" project. That way you won't leave out an important step. Try to fit your instructions into six steps.

☐ Fill in the Oral Report Cue Cards

Use your organizer as a guide. The cards are numbered at the top. Write them in order.

Topic sentences are on the cards to help you. If you have more than six steps cut more cards and write your own numbers at the top.

After you have written all the steps, cut the cards apart and put them in numerical order.

☐ Practice your demonstration aloud

Use the cards as cues to help you remember what to say. Practice at least five times so that you can easily speak and demonstrate at the same time.

Now you're ready! Collect all your materials. Get the cue cards in order. Speak in a loud, clear voice. Good Luck!

Oral Report Organizer

What are you going to demonstrate?

_____

_____

List all materials and ingredients needed for the demonstration.

_____

_____

_____

List the steps in the order they are needed to complete the demonstration.

1. _____

_____

2. _____

_____

3. _____

_____

4. _____

_____

5. _____

_____

6. _____

_____

If there are more than six steps list them below.

_____

_____

_____

_____

Report Form Roundup © *Edupress*

Cue Cards

1. Today I am going to show you how to

_____

_____

_____

_____

(Explain what you will demonstrate.)

2. To do this you will need

_____

_____

_____

_____

(Name all materials and ingredients.)

3. The first step is

_____

_____

_____

_____

4. Next you _____

_____

_____

_____

_____

Cue Cards

5. After that is finished your next step is

_____

_____

_____

_____

_____

6. Progress is being made! Now you

_____

_____

_____

_____

_____

7. The final step is _____

_____

_____

_____

8. Now you've seen how to _____

_____

_____

(Tell again what your demonstration was.)

Are you ready to try it yourself?

Report Form Roundup © _Edupress_

Keeping the Report Records

To the teacher...

The report records on the following pages will aid in tracking student progress and provide another means of communication between you, your students and their parents.

To use the records you will need to:
- Reproduce a set for each child.
- Reproduce the letter below plus the level descriptions on page 2 for the parents.
- Provide a folder for each student for safekeeping of report records and parent correspondence.

You may decide to have children complete only some of the reports. Choose from a variety of levels so that skill progression can take place.

To complete the report records you will need to:
- Check off report tasks as they are completed. Indicate work turned in late.
- Indicate grades earned. You may want to do this for each phase plus the overall grade.
- Write comments and suggestions.
- Send the record home for parent review and feedback.

- -

To the parents...

Your child will be working on the development of research, fact-finding and reporting skills. In order to track progress, a report record will be maintained.

On this record you will find the following information:
- Report topic and level (see attached for level descriptions)
- Checklist of completed tasks
- Performance grade(s)
- Teacher comments and suggestions
- A box for parent initial

If you would like to comment on any report, please do so on a separate paper. We will store this correspondence in your child's report folder.

Thank you for your support.

Student Name_____ # Report Records

Report Topic	Level	Fact Sheet	Report Project	Grade	Extra Credit	Teacher Comments	Parent Initial
Autobiography	A						
My Family	B						
My School	A						
My Classroom	A						
Hobby	B						
My Favorite Holiday	B						
Local Current Event	A						
Front Page News	A						
Sports Current Event	A						
Weather Report	A						
National Weather Report	A						
Movie Review	A						
Television Show Review	A						
Restaurant Review	A						
Visit My Community	A						
Community Newsletter	B						
Interview	C						
Fiction Book	A						
Non-Fiction Book	A						
Mystery Book	A						

Student Name_____ # Report Records

Report Topic	Level	Fact Sheet	Report Project	Grade	Extra Credit	Teacher Comments	Parent Initial
Fairy Tale	B						
Legend	B						
Athlete	B						
World Leader	B						
Biography	C						
State or Province	C						
Country	C						
Desert	B						
Continent	B						
Mountain	B						
Natural Wonders	B						
Capital City	C						
Musical Instrument	A						
Sport	B						
Bird	B						
Insect	B						
Flower	C						
Animal	C						
Planet	B						
Invention	B						
Oral Report	C						